HAVE
NO
FEAR

HAVE
NO
FEAR

BEING SALT AND LIGHT
EVEN WHEN IT'S COSTLY

JOHN C. LENNOX

Unless otherwise stated, Scripture quotations are from The Holy Bible,
English Standard Version, published by HarperCollins*Publishers*
© 2001 by Crossway Bibles, a division of Good News Publishers.
Used by permission. All rights reserved.

Copyright © 2018 by John C. Lennox
First published in Great Britain in 2018 and reprinted 2019

The right of John C. Lennox to be identified as the Author of this Work
has been asserted by him in accordance with the Copyright, Designs
and Patents Act 1988.

British Library Cataloguing in Publication Data
A record for this book is available from the British Library

ISBN: 978-1-912373-61-1

Designed and typeset by Pete Barnsley (CreativeHoot.com)

Printed in Denmark by Nørhaven

10Publishing, a division of 10ofthose.com
Unit C, Tomlinson Road, Leyland, PR25 2DY, England

Email: info@10ofthose.com
Website: www.10ofthose.com

DEDICATION

For Richard and Jane Borgonon
in gratitude for their friendship and
partnership over many years.

CONTENTS

INTRODUCTION

Jesus said that his followers were 'the salt of the earth' and 'the light of the world' (Matthew 5:13–14). They were to have a profound influence on the society in which they lived, being a salty preservative to stem decay and blazing a path for others to follow. That is, their lives were to be active, not passive. They were to be Jesus' witnesses to the world by how they lived and what they said. Those two things belonged together – what they said would only be credible if it was also modelled in their lives; and people would only understand their lives and the motivation for them if they spoke about and explained this. Jesus' disciples were to be characterised by living out their faith in public, rather than keeping their faith private. They were to prove their authenticity as Christians by deliberately and willingly swimming against the stream.

That doesn't mean they were never afraid. Indeed, Peter denied he even knew Jesus when a girl challenged him at the time of Jesus' trial. He became so scared he swore black and blue that he did not have anything to do with Jesus.

Yet a few weeks later, when hostile religious authorities tried to censor the apostles, the same Peter said, 'we cannot but speak of what we have seen and heard' (Acts 4:20). They were not going to be silenced. Later Peter wrote to his fellow Christians everywhere and so to us: 'always being prepared to make a defence to anyone who asks you for a reason for the hope that is in you' (1 Peter 3:15).

Yet many of us don't feel always prepared. If we are honest, some of us don't really feel ready at all. We get scared of what people might say. The pressure to silence the public witness of Christians has not gone away. It is very real. Indeed, in many parts of the world the secular and religious opposition has intensified to the extent that, particularly in the West, the dominant attitude is that religion is a private business and should be kept that way. As a result, many Christians have been effectively silenced.

They may well continue to go to church but their witness has long since ceased because of fear and peer pressure.

I experienced this pressure very early on as a student. At a formal college dinner I found myself sitting beside a Nobel Prize winner. I had never met one before and, in order to gain the most from the conversation, I tried to ask him questions. For example, how had his science shaped his worldview, and what was his big picture of the status and meaning of the universe? In particular, I was interested in whether his wide-ranging studies had led him to reflect on the existence of God.

It was clear that he was not comfortable with that question so I immediately backed off. However, at the end of the meal he invited me to come to his study. He had also invited two or three other senior academics but no other students. I was invited to sit and, so far as I recall, they remained standing.

He began, 'Lennox, do you want a career in science?'

'Yes, sir,' I replied.

'Then,' he said, 'in front of witnesses, tonight,

you must give up this childish faith in God. If you do not, then it will cripple you intellectually and you will suffer by comparison with your peers. You simply will not make it.'[1]

Talk about pressure! I had never experienced anything like it before. What does one do when faced with this kind of situation? But it does not take a brilliant scientist to create this sort of pressure and intimidation. A sarcastic remark about our faith in God from a teacher at school can be enough to embarrass us in front of our classmates. Even worse are posts on social media making fun of what we believe. They can make us hesitant or even ashamed and fearful of putting our heads above the parapet and aligning ourselves with Jesus Christ.

It is hard to swim against the flow. What can help us do it?

The purpose of this little book is to demonstrate that you – yes, you – can actually be a faithful witness to Jesus. Furthermore, this is not some grim task that you do because you feel guilty. Instead, it will bring you a great sense of joy and strengthen your Christian life and experience immeasurably.

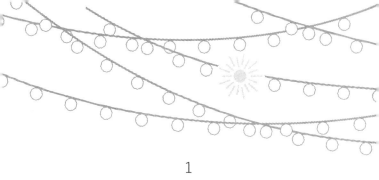

1

GETTING STARTED

We've already seen, in 1 Peter 3:15, that Peter urges all Christians to be constantly ready to explain their faith. As we begin to look at evangelism in detail, it is helpful to look carefully at the context of this command:

> *Now who is there to harm you if you are zealous for what is good? But even if you should suffer for righteousness' sake, you will be blessed. Have no fear of them, nor be troubled, but in your hearts regard Christ the Lord as holy, always being prepared to make a defence to anyone who asks you for a reason for the hope that is in you; yet do it with gentleness and respect, having a good conscience, so that, when you are slandered, those who revile*

*your good behaviour in Christ may be put to
shame. For it is better to suffer for doing good,
if that should be God's will, than for doing evil*
(1 Peter 3:13–17).

Peter's mention of fear is a good place to start
since many people find witnessing initially
quite scary. Peter personally knew about fear
as a Christian, as we have also seen. He was
writing to people who were feeling intimidated
and insecure, and had good reason to do so. Yet
instead of telling them to keep their heads down,
he commands them, 'in your hearts regard
Christ the Lord as holy, always being prepared
to make a defence to anyone who asks you for a
reason for the hope that is in you' (v. 15).

The antidote to fear is not so much in our
store of answers to possible questions that might
arise but is first of all in our attitude to our Lord.
We are to honour him as Lord. We are also to
remember that he is 'holy', which means 'set
apart'. Peter is explaining that we prepare to
engage in witness by deliberately focussing on
Jesus' Lordship – of the world as well as of how
we should live our lives. In this way a wrong

kind of fear – of others – is dispelled by the right kind of 'fear': of the Lord.

We are to be Jesus' ambassadors, by our words and actions. Yet we are not alone in this. Jesus promised his disciples – and us – that he would send the Holy Spirit to bear the major burden of witness: 'But when the Helper comes, whom I will send to you from the Father, the Spirit of truth, who proceeds from the Father, he will bear witness about me. And you also will bear witness' (John 15:26–27). Jesus is in charge, encouraging us to witness. We need to get this straight, and can expect to have conversations about Jesus since he is more interested in other people than we are. Jesus is also present with us, by his Spirit, to guide our conversations and help us in all our uncertainties and fears.

CONVERSATION

Notice next in this passage that Peter is not talking about preaching – that is an ability that most of us do not have. He envisages a situation where someone else asks us about our Christian hope. That is, he is talking about a one-to-one chat. While this is public in one sense, it is only between the two of you. That ought to make you feel a little more comfortable already!

It is one-to-one conversations that are the key to Christian witness. Notice too that it is *not* us who starts this conversation: we are to answer 'anyone who asks you for a reason for the hope that is in you' (v. 15). That is helpful because many of us stumble at the first hurdle: we don't know how to start conversations about Jesus and so we never do.

However, you may be wondering why anyone would ask you about your Christian hope. I remember many years ago asking myself the same question. I had reached the stage where I thought I was ready to answer at least some questions about the Christian faith, yet no one asked me and so Peter's statement seemed rather ineffective and useless. I shared my problem with a younger student friend, who at once replied, 'Have you ever thought of asking them about their hope?'

'No,' I said.

'Why not?'

'Well, it's obvious that many of them have no hope, so there is no point in asking them!'

'Really?' he questioned. 'Try it.'

Not long after that I was on a train to London and found myself sitting beside a middle-aged man who was reading a scientific-looking text. I uttered, 'Hello, are you a scientist.'

'Yes, I am a metallurgist. How about you?'

'I'm studying mathematics.'

The conversation then lapsed. He continued his reading. I took out a Gideon New Testament and started to read it. Yet he noticed what I was doing (as I hoped!) and eventually said, 'Pardon me, but is that a New Testament you are reading?'

'Yes,' I said simply, and continued to read.

After a while he broke in once more: 'I don't wish to disturb you, but you did say you were a maths student, and yet here you are reading the Bible. How is that possible?' I then remembered the advice I had received from my friend. I answered, 'You want to know why I am reading the Bible? Tell me, have you got any hope?'

The effect was dramatic. He turned white and mumbled something about us all 'muddling through'. I said, 'You know I didn't mean that. I meant, do you have any personal hope?'

'None whatsoever,' he replied. 'Do you, and what is it?'

There it was – the question that Peter said would start the conversation. And it has started a multitude of others since then.

The essence of my conversation with this man teaches us two simple steps about how to witness to Jesus. First of all, I observed something about the man: the science text he was reading. Next, I asked a question related to it: 'Are you a scientist?'

ASKING QUESTIONS

One of my heroes from the ancient world is the Greek philosopher Socrates, who was famous for the fact that he went around asking questions. Unfortunately, this got him into trouble for he was accused of corrupting the minds of the youth of Athens. The court sentenced him to death by suicide – an inexcusable tragedy. Please don't let that put you off asking questions! I learned very early two things: firstly, that it is much easier to ask questions than to answer them; and secondly, that questions are a great way to get into conversation with people – whether friends or strangers – and know them better.

Indeed, I have found that one of the best ways to proceed in chats with people, especially with those you have not met before, is to keep asking them questions until they ask you one. Of course, some of us might find that stressful since we have too much to say!

What sort of questions should we ask in order to have the opportunity to speak naturally of our Christian faith? We should begin with ordinary questions so that we can get to know them and learn how to build bridges with them. Therefore, ask them about their family, interests and job. At the same time be careful in case they might not be married, have children or be in a job – you may be in danger of giving the false impression that their family situation or job defines them. Of course, you may rapidly find that you share a common hobby or interest, for instance playing a particular sport, supporting the same football team, cooking or enjoying going on walks. Discussion will then rapidly flow.

This general questioning process might be enough for our first conversations together. During them we should be listening out for their questions about our faith, and when they arise, we need to take them seriously. We also need to be sensitive. For example, we may have had a loving father and so, as a Christian, can well understand what it means to have God as Father. But the person we are talking to may have been abused by their father and therefore may completely fail to understand us when we try to tell them what God being a Father means. We must constantly remind ourselves that we don't all come from the same background; what might encourage one person may upset another. Christ must be central – not us and our experience.

Let me give you another example of conversation starting. Once, when I was waiting for a flight, the man next to me was constantly interrupted by his mobile phone ringing. I could hear his responses – they were all terse instructions in how to deal with particular medical cases. He was quite agitated. So in one of the pauses I commented, 'Does your work always chase you like that?'

Relieved to have someone to talk to, he replied, 'I am afraid so. It would seem I am always on call. Is your life like that?'

'Not really, I am glad to say. I am a teacher in a university.'

'Are you? I have a son at university and I am really worried about him. He is very lonely and is not getting much help to integrate with the others. Are there any resources to help students have hope in that kind of situation.'

There it was again: that word 'hope'. I could see that our flight was about to be called so I cut straight to the point and answered, 'May I be very personal since we don't have much time. I have in the end found that what gives me a hope that I can share with others is a living relationship with God. That is, my hope comes through trusting my life, with all its ups and downs and concerns, to Jesus Christ. Now that may well sound like so much jargon to you but you can find out all about it by reading the New Testament. Would you permit me to give you a New Testament to pass on to your son? Please also encourage him to get in touch with the Christian group in his university which he will easily find – it is called the Universities and Colleges Christian Fellowship (UCCF). He will find friendly students there who will be able to help.'

'Thank you very much,' he replied. 'Would you mind if I read it too while I am on holiday?'

I never heard from him again. That often happens with brief encounters with strangers. I simply trusted the Lord that I had been a link in a chain to this man discovering the Christian hope, though the details of it I may never know – at least in this world.

I learned about this matter of trusting the Lord in the context of being a witness in my early days as a student. Another student had asked to talk to me about my faith in Christ. However, I was rather nervous about doing so and therefore, with his permission, I invited another Christian student, Stuart, to join us. (This was the same person who had told me to ask people about their hope!) Before the other student returned, Stuart prayed with words that I have often used since: 'Lord, we pray that you will give us wisdom and help in this conversation to say what you want us to say: no less and no more.'

I put on some coffee and Stuart started the conversation by making a remark about his home football team, Preston North End. Instantly, a passionate discussion began and I discovered that there is much more to the world of football than I had ever imagined! Once Stuart had put him at his ease in this way, Stuart then moved to the question that had motivated the student to come to see me in the first place: 'You would like to talk about faith in Christ. How can we help?' The student was remarkably open with his questions and Stuart readily answered them, finally asking him if he would like to become a Christian there and then. 'Is that possible?' he asked. 'It is indeed,' Stuart replied, and led him in a prayer of commitment. And so in this instance, and in God's kindness, a new Christian was born that day in my room.

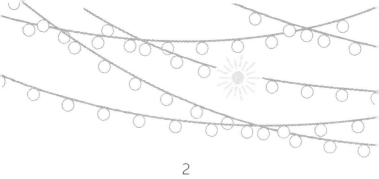

2

MAKING A
DEFENCE

Another aspect Peter speaks about, in
1 Peter 3:15, is that we must always be ready
'to make a defence to anyone who asks you
for a reason for the hope that is in you'. The
word 'defence' is a translation of the Greek
word *apologia*, from which we derive the word
'apologetics'. We need to establish that this
association is unfortunate for two reasons.
Firstly, it can sound as if we are apologising for
our Christian faith, which is absolutely not the
case. Secondly, apologetics is now thought by
many to be a highly intellectual activity only
to be engaged in by the cleverest of Christians.
That is dangerously misleading. Of course, we

are all grateful to intellectually gifted Christians who can explain difficult issues that most of us cannot. For those reasons I tend to avoid the word 'apologetics' and replace it with what is actually meant here: persuasive evangelism. This is what all Christians are called upon to do, not just a few bright sparks, and is the meaning of Peter urging us 'to make defence'.

In the book of Acts we see several examples of Paul giving such an *apologia*. In each case he is not answering subtle, complex intellectual questions, but telling the story of his encounter with the risen Lord Jesus on the road to Damascus from Jerusalem. He is speaking about how this changed his life and filled him with new purpose and hope. That is, he talks about his experience of the Lord. All of us can do the same and explain how we came to accept Jesus as our Lord and Saviour, and therefore also where our hope lies.

Having explained the essence of our Christian hope, we will find that people want to hear the reasons behind such a belief – as Peter says. After all, we cannot open our mouths about our experience of Christ in a pluralistic, multicultural, broadly secular society these days without running the risk of being misunderstood, misrepresented or even opposed in unpleasant ways. Because that is the case, all of us will have to actively defend what we believe by giving reasons for our beliefs.

Some Christians get a bit bothered at this point. They question whether we should not be trusting the Holy Spirit to reveal the truth of the gospel to people, rather than trusting our reason. This gives the false impression that revelation and reason are opposed to each other. The apostle Paul was a towering genius and went around reasoning with all he met – in synagogues, market places and anywhere else that people gathered (see, for example, Acts 17:22–31). But the secret of his effectiveness was that he used his reason *and* trusted God to be at work bringing people to faith. The danger for some of us, especially if we have been privileged to have a good education, is that we are tempted to trust mostly our reason, relying on God's power to work only when we get stuck. It is that kind of thinking that we should fear. Reason and revelation are not in themselves opposed –

I have never yet met anyone who can read the revelation of God that is his Word, the Bible, without using their reason.

WHAT IF WE GET STUCK?

That neatly brings me to the inevitable question: what do we do if we get stuck? One of the hurdles we will all face is not being able to answer a particular question. Some people are especially worried that they are not suitably gifted or trained to witness to others. However, the reality is that none of us knows everything. Yet we can have a strategy for coping with such occasions, for example when we are confronted with a question we haven't thought about before.

First of all, it is vital to be honest. We should admit our inability to answer right away. It's helpful to then explain that you will go away and investigate their question and will come back to them with what you find out. You will never lose face by explaining that you don't know the answer. In fact, your response tells your conversation partner several important things about you. Firstly, you don't claim to know everything. Secondly, you take their question seriously. Thirdly, you would like to see them again and discuss their question.

Next, we need to make every effort to answer their question. We should take time to think it through with the help of God's Word, as well as by seeking help from relevant Christian books or from other Christians. Then, once we have done so, we will not easily forget it. This is key to learning how to witness. While, of course, it is good to benefit from the knowledge of others and to read books on Christian apologetics, they can often lead to despair because, if we are honest, we forget what we have read. This may happen especially when we read answers to questions that are not of immediate relevance and so are not memorable. It is far better to spend most of our time on seeking answers to questions that are real to us, having arisen in the course of our conversations.

Of course, answering questions that we find difficult will be costly in terms of our time and energy. However, if we take our faith in the Lord seriously, we will do the work with joy. Then it will be a great encouragement to us when we see that our efforts have paid off and our answers make sense when we next meet our conversation partners.

By contrast, we will lose face if we pretend to have an answer when we clearly don't. The word 'agnostic' means 'a person who does not know'. We are all agnostic about many things. That means we can all learn. In fact, 'learner' is the meaning of the word 'disciple'.

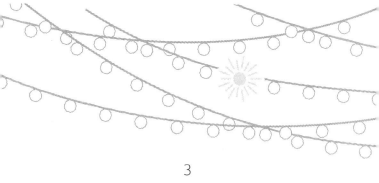

3

CONVERSING ABOUT JESUS

There is one way of witnessing that we should always bear in mind. Jesus said, 'everyone who acknowledges me ... I also will acknowledge' (Matthew 10:32). An acknowledgement is usually very short, so this verse suggests that we can witness by briefly acknowledging the Lord in a conversation. We can then see if our conversation partner picks up on this comment. If they don't, we leave our remark without making an issue of it.

For instance, perhaps we are chatting with someone about the news when they say something about an awful disaster or terrorist act. We might ask, 'Do you think faith in God can help people in such situations?' If they follow up on our remark, then we can continue. If they do not, we can just let it go. Another opportunity will arise.

It is important to know when to let things go. We Christians are sometimes in danger of being so passionate about our message – which is understandable – that we fail to be sensitive to the negative reaction of those listening to us. Therefore here are some things to bear in mind.

Firstly, we should be careful not to acquire a reputation as a 'monomaniac' – someone who can only talk about one thing – and therefore get put down as a 'religious nut'. If we want people to be interested in what we have to say, out of love for them, we need to converse with them about other subjects. We must not be a one-track person. If we feel that we have too few interests to make us an interesting conversation partner, we should find some more! At the very least we can read a newspaper or listen to the news so that we can chat about the wider world.

Secondly, when we sense someone is beginning to feel 'got at', we should not press the point but move on. That is, we must always be prepared to give the other person space. We need to judge when they have had enough – and before they tell us so.

The key thing is not to let ourselves get under pressure to 'give a message'. Not only will that prove intimidating but we will fail to communicate the gospel effectively. However, sometimes things are taken out of our hands.

This happened to me once. Sitting at a meal with a group of young people – some Christians and some not – I was asked by the person beside me why I believed in the resurrection of Jesus. I answered but tried to keep my voice down. However, that had the very opposite effect to the one I wanted – the buzz of conversation at the table died down and all were listening. Finally, one man further down the table could stand it no more. He hammered his knife on the table and shouted, 'Stop that nonsense – I have never heard such rubbish in my life.'

There was dead silence as they waited for me to say something. I commented (trying to give myself space to think!), 'You seem to feel very strongly about this.'

'You bet I do,' he said.

'In that case, I would be interested to know what you made of the evidence for the resurrection given in the New Testament when you studied it ...'

'I, well, I didn't know there was any,' he spluttered.

The meal was over and I invited him to my room for coffee. He was open enough to ask about this evidence for the resurrection. After a while, I paused the conversation by enquiring, 'Suppose I could provide enough evidence to demonstrate that Jesus did rise from the dead and was the Son of God as he claimed. Tell me, would you be prepared to take the step of trusting him for salvation?'

'No,' he said, 'my parents shoved this stuff down my throat when I was at home, and I just don't want anything to do with it!'

'Thanks for being honest,' I replied, 'for that is really the first honest thing you have said to me all evening.'

The conversation at once changed in tone as he told me about the resentment he had against this 'religious stuff' pushed into him. It was not long before he realised that there was a rational way to approach the Christian faith without emotional blackmail. Wonderfully, once he saw this, it was not long before he became a Christian.

This example shows that sometimes people's initial reactions and even their questions are driven by emotion and experience rather than reason. We have to be sensitive enough to tell the difference and address the questioner more than the question. Of course, not all reactions are like this. Treat questions as genuine unless there is good reason to think otherwise.

HOSTING DISCUSSION EVENTS

Another way of getting conversation going is to invite people to a meal and to watch something interesting on TV or the Internet. The meal does not necessarily have to be elaborate. In fact for this purpose something simple is best.

When I was a student, we had very little technology. However, I did have a reel-to-reel tape recorder (how primitive it seems nowadays – most of you have probably never seen one!) and recordings of a series of lectures called 'The Case for Belief'. These were by my friend and mentor, Professor David Gooding, and in them he dealt with various objections to Christianity. I would simply tell my guests that I had found the talk interesting and would play a short extract which we would then discuss. The response was excellent and some very fruitful conversations ensued.

There is so much more material available today, such as podcasts, that can be used for the same purpose. Especially useful are those that have interactions between, say, Christians and atheists – since both sides are represented, people are much more willing to listen because they are less likely to feel 'got at'. One very good source is Premier Christian Radio's podcasts of their show *Unbelievable* with Justin Brierley, which is an apologetics and theology debate programme.[2] There are many others easily to be found on the Internet.

I am aware that some people take fright at the idea of this kind of thing. A common reaction is: 'I would be too scared to do that because I have no skill at leading a discussion.' My response is who said you had to lead a discussion? If you invite a mixed group of people and together listen to or watch something interesting, there will be a discussion whether or not you say anything. We need to get right out of our heads the notion that anything like this all depends on our ability to lead a discussion. It doesn't. Instead, trust the Lord and be willing to take a risk by doing something along these lines. Witnessing is like swimming. You will never be sure the water will hold you up until you commit yourself and get into it. Take the plunge to witness and you will find that the Lord will hold you up as he has promised.

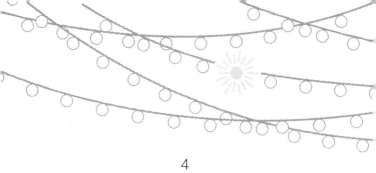

4

THE USE OF SCRIPTURE IN WITNESSING

Implicit in all that I have said so far is that in expressing our hope and giving reasons for it we shall constantly refer to the Bible. However, while it is one thing to quote relevant biblical passages in conversation, it is another to have a one-to-one chat with Scripture itself as the central focus.

It is the entrance of the Word of God into a person's heart that brings light and understanding. So our priority as witnesses should be to bring our friends and acquaintances into direct contact with Scripture. This is particularly so since contemporary society is increasingly biblically illiterate. However, many Christians, though they see the importance of introducing people to Scripture, will readily admit that they have no idea how to start doing this. Hence they are embarrassed even to suggest it. Overcoming this hurdle is our next step.

As this difficulty is well-known, there have been many attempts to answer it in the form of various Bible reading programmes. Many of these are good and helpful studies that will help you to read the Bible with a friend evangelistically. You may already have a favourite resource – like Christianity Explored – and I would encourage you to continue to use what you have found most helpful in opening up Scripture with your friends. Since it is not yet so well-known, I am going to focus here on a resource called *The Word: One to One* which can be looked at as an excellent introduction to other evangelistic courses. It is also a very user-friendly way of helping you get alongside your friends in a one-to-one conversation about the Bible.[3] Its idea is deceptively simple but there is ample evidence that it is bearing a great deal of fruit around the world among people of all ages, stages and educational abilities.

The Word: One to One is a series of Bible notes designed to introduce your friends to Jesus in the Gospel of John. With a copy each, you and your conversation partner read the material together. The biblical text is printed and therefore open in front of you. Also included in the notes are a series of questions that help you understand what John is saying. The unique feature of this series is it gives not only questions but also the answers to them, thus eliminating the threat of potential embarrassment on both sides.

Experience has shown that people, even busy people, are more willing to sit down with their Christian friends and read the Bible than those friends might think. Furthermore, the relationships that are developed through reading together are strong and lasting. Here are some examples of people's experiences using these notes to give you some idea of their value:

In North London, a lively teenage girl came up to me in great excitement because her brother had just agreed to do the first 'episode' of the notes. Her minister told me later that he had buried her father, a hopeless alcoholic, and that both her mother and her brother were drug users. The girl herself had been so disruptive that she had regularly been thrown out of the youth club. However, she found The Word: One to One *socially accessible to her and she had been solidly converted through reading John in that way. She was now sharing the notes with her school friends.*

One man who worked in the insurance industry used *The Word: One to One* to share the Bible with many of his colleagues. His friend slammed his desk on their third meeting and asked, 'How is it possible that I can have had one of the most expensive educations that money can buy yet no one has ever shown me this?!' What that Christian has found through sharing Scripture is that it becomes self-authenticating to the people you read it with:

The smartest man I ever led to the Lord took fifteen months to make that commitment. When I asked what had brought him to the foot of the cross, he quipped, 'Well, it was nothing that you said! In fact, I don't remember what you said, but I couldn't get out of mind what the Word said, in particular the first six words of John's Gospel: 'In the beginning was the Word'! Those words went into my mind like a branding iron on meat. 'In the beginning ...' I thought, Richard Dawkins, you are wrong, there has to have been a beginning. The more I read John's Gospel, the more it showed me who the Word was, what he came to do, how he died on the cross so that I might live, and that he rose again so that I might be adopted into his family for eternity. My becoming a Christian was nothing to do with what you said, but because of what John said.

The man who told his Christian friend that his conversion was not about him was making an important point that can take some of the unnecessary stress out of our witness. We can easily get over-concerned about how we look, about the impression we make, about how people think about us. These things are not unimportant – we do not wish to appear boorish, or unkind, or unthoughtful. But we need to focus on trusting the Lord for he is the one who has promised to make our witness effective: 'I chose you and appointed you that you should go and bear fruit' (John 15:16). He is the centre of the message; we are not.

Elderly people have found *The Word: One to One* a wonderful resource that has brought a completely new dimension into their lives. One man of eighty-nine was using the notes with seven people because he had discovered that so many of his friends were not at peace. A seventy-eight-year-old widow was asked by a lady in her church if she had the time to visit her aged mother. Instead of taking chocolates or flowers, she took *The Word: One to One*. The ninety-year-old mother knew she was not at peace and was solidly converted.

Whatever a person's age or circumstances, a Christian friend of mine helpfully summarises the way in which many come to understand what the Gospel is:

A friend after a few weeks said with a smile,
'I realise now that I got it all wrong! I thought

being a Christian was about doing good but actually it's all been done for me. All I have to do is believe.' Versions of this are extremely common. Indeed, most of our friends don't understand the Christian message at all and think it only consists of moral teaching. It's not that our friends have considered the Christian message and rejected it; it's often that they haven't understood it in the first place. Opening up the Bible and reading it with friends one-to-one is like a light bulb being turned on.

I hope you find these testimonies an encouragement to you to get going and ask a friend to read the Bible with you. The Word of God is alive and active and will work in your friends' lives when you open up the Bible with them whatever method or resource you decide to use. If you'd like to try using *The Word: One to One* then first of all, watch the introduction to using the notes on YouTube given by the evangelist Rico Tice of All Souls, Langham Place in London.[4] Next, look at the website – https://www.theword121.com – to learn how to get the resource itself, including the option of downloading it for free. There you will also find tips on how to use it, frequently asked questions and more stories of those who have already benefitted from it.

Having said all this, we should remember that many people have come to faith in Christ through reading Scripture without any contact with anyone else. The work of Gideons International – placing New Testaments in hotels, schools, universities, prisons, hospitals and so on – is ample proof of that. In light of this I make it a practice whenever possible, and particularly when travelling, to carry a Gideon New Testament with me. I pray each time that I may be able to give it to someone who will read it. I must say that I find it odd that there are many Christians who would say that they believe the Bible is the Word of God but who never think of giving a portion of it away. When did you last share the Bible with a friend?

5

WALKING THE TALK

Our character plays a major role in all our witnessing. No one will be interested in what we say unless they can see that our lives back up what we profess to believe. We need to walk the talk.

Jesus commanded us to be 'the salt of the earth' and 'the light of the world' (Matthew 5:13–14), as we saw in the introduction. Matthew 5:16 continues, 'In the same way, let your light shine before others, so that they may see your good works and give glory to your Father who is in heaven.' Peter makes the reverse point. We are to engage with people: 'with gentleness and respect, having a good conscience, so that, when you are slandered, those who revile your good behaviour in Christ may be put to shame. For it is better to suffer for doing good, if that should be God's will, than for doing evil' (1 Peter 3:16–17).

Given the importance of our conduct as Christians, it is vital we put each of Peter's instructions into practice.

GENTLENESS

We all have different temperaments. As a result, some of us find it easier to be gentle than others – while others can tend towards being too gentle or timid. We have to learn to change our character where necessary. As Christians, we have the power of God's Spirit in our lives to transform us into his likeness.

We claim that Jesus is our Lord. The way people will see that is when our character reflects that of Jesus. As we study the Gospels, we see how gentle a witness he was, particularly with people whose lives were raw and hopeless. His gentleness did not mean that he was never firm – he was very firm with religious bigots who opposed his message. However, he constantly showed an awareness of and concern for people's problems.

He showed such compassion to hurting people that they responded by sharing their problems with him and by becoming open to his message.

RESPECT

The next quality Peter lists – respect – is something my parents taught me by their example. I was a teenager in Northern Ireland at a time when the Troubles were looming. There was a sectarian divide in the population. Yet because my father believed that all men and women were made in the image of God, irrespective of what they believed, he was even-handed in his approach to hiring staff in his store. That was a dangerous thing to do, as subsequent terrorist bombs proved. However, my father put his convictions first. I never forgot the lesson.

Some people find it hard to treat with respect those who disagree with them. That attitude is even more difficult to understand when it is found among professing Christian believers. If we are going to engage with others, we need to bend over backwards to show our respect. This does not mean papering over differences and disagreements. Like Paul we should proclaim, 'I am not ashamed of the gospel, for it is the power of God for salvation to everyone who believes' (Romans 1:16).

The apostle Paul says that we should 'speak the truth in love' (Ephesians 4:15). Speaking the truth is easy if we do not have to love people. Being sentimental with people and 'loving' them is easy if we avoid speaking the truth. It is doing both simultaneously that is the challenge. Yet, if our witness is to be effective, we must learn to do so and build this quality into our characters. We need to work at this, but it is possible with God's help.

It is even harder to show respect if people revile us, as Peter warns that they will (1 Peter 3:16). We shall have to learn to rely on the Lord to help us suppress that powerful desire to 'get our own back' or 'give as good as we get'. At the same time we need to do this in such a way that we don't come across as insipid, weak and having lost the courage of our convictions.

HAVING A GOOD CONSCIENCE

There is a moral side to our witness. The particular thing Peter has in mind here is the fact that Christians are likely to be misrepresented and slandered – or even persecuted. We must never give any grounds for false accusation. This is especially relevant now as we live in a world that is increasingly given to slander of all kinds. These range from vicious comments on social media that sometimes destroy people's lives to public accusations of impropriety.

As Christians we are not claiming to be better than other people. We are sinners. However, if we trust Jesus as our Saviour – if we believe he died on the cross to take the punishment for our sin – we know that we are forgiven. With Jesus as our Lord, we also know that we have now received a new power in our lives.

If that is true, then there must be perceptible change in the way we conduct our lives. If we are perceived to cheat, lust, lie, gossip, steal or show envy and anger, our message will not be heard but rather ridiculed. Remember that we are trying to get across to people the wonder of salvation. It is impossible to do that if our lives look anything other than 'saved'.

God has given each of us a conscience that is, at any given time, our best guide to right and wrong. If that conscience is niggling at us, we need to take action. Perhaps there are things in our lives and relationships that we need to get sorted out. Maybe we must ask forgiveness from those we have wronged. Others of us will need to wage war in particular areas of our lives, for example cleaning up our Internet activities. Otherwise we shall not have the desire, let alone the energy, to witness to our faith in Christ.

SUFFERING FOR DOING GOOD

Peter is realistic about the Christian experience. In his day, he saw trouble for Christians on the horizon – beginning with sporadic harassment by the authorities but leading in some cases to active persecution and physical suffering. He tells his fellow believers elsewhere in this letter (1 Peter 4:12) that they should not be surprised by such troubles. Jesus 'suffered in the flesh' (1 Peter 4:1) and they may have to walk in his painful steps.

Our society is no different. Many believers are having to cope with a dominant secularism that wishes to push any religious convictions into the private sphere. It actively resists our attempts to witness. Others around the world are suffering acute persecution. We too need to remember that the Lord was there before us: 'If the world hates you, know that it has hated me before it hated you' (John 15:18). We should also remember that the Greek word for 'witness' is the word from which we get 'martyr' – witnessing about Jesus will inevitably bring suffering.

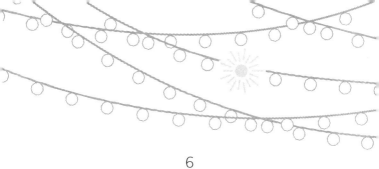

6

THE DIFFERENCE BETWEEN RELIGION AND CHRISTIANITY

People often make the mistake of thinking that Christianity is a religion like any other. I have found it very interesting to ask many people what they think religion actually is. The general consensus is that religion is a way of relating human beings to something beyond themselves, something transcendent. It usually consists of a ritual of initiation and then a path to be followed on the basis of prescribed teaching. Religious ceremonies and holy buildings are considered important. The ultimate focus, entry into the world to come, is thought dependent on a final assessment of one's life based on merit gained on the path.

It is that understanding of things that leads people to say, 'I'm just as good a Christian as anybody else. I do no one any harm. I cannot understand why you say I need saving? Why do you keep talking about sin?' My response to that is perhaps best communicated by telling the following story – after all I am Irish!

A number of years ago I was making my way home after teaching in a church in Hungary. I was travelling by train to Vienna, via Budapest, in order to catch a flight home. I found my reserved seat in a second-class carriage and sat down. At once, I began unaccountably to feel uneasy about the seat I was in – an experience I had never had before, nor indeed since. I first thought that perhaps I was in the wrong seat but a glance at my ticket showed that was not the case. It then occurred to me that I should go and sit in first class. This conviction became so strong that I left the carriage, walked to the front of the train and found there were two first-class carriages – one was shabby and old; the other seemed brand new. As the train was about to leave, I tried to get into the shiny new carriage. However, bizarrely, I found I could not move one leg in front of the other. I began to panic, thinking I was having some kind of seizure. But when I turned towards the shabby carriage, I found I could move, and so I dived in just as the train pulled out of the station.

I just about fell into the seat near the door of the compartment – the two window seats were occupied. At once I felt relaxed and normal again but very puzzled by what had happened. I closed my eyes to get some rest. Then I became aware of two men in the window seats speaking quietly to each other in a language I could not understand.

After a while they changed to French, which I could understand and speak. Now recovered, I wished them good day and we chatted a little about our respective jobs. They were both senior international lawyers: one an ambassador; the other a judge from an international court. I explained I was a mathematician.

The conversation lapsed and I was beginning to doze off when one of them suddenly exclaimed, *'Voyez, les croix!'* ('Look at the crosses!') He pointed at a cemetery through the window and then asked, 'Are there Christians in this country?' I replied by telling them that there were indeed many Christians, and I had been spending a week with some of them, teaching them from the Bible.

'But that is not rational,' came the reply. 'You are a mathematician. How can you possibly take the Bible seriously? And, in any case, we can approach God directly, even in the desert. We don't need intermediaries like Jesus and Mary to help us.'

After more conversation, during which I said that my Christian faith was evidence-based, one of them said to me, 'We have three hours on this train. Would you be prepared to explain to us the difference between Christianity and our religion?'

I asked them what the essence of their religion was and then I looked around for paper and pen to illustrate my answer. Not finding any, I noticed that the floor of the carriage was quite dusty, and so I was able to draw on it with my finger the following diagram. As I did so, I asked, 'Would it be fair to say that your religion amounts to this?'

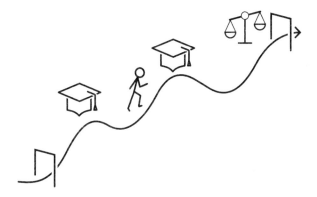

I continued, 'In most religions there is a door of initiation at the beginning – perhaps a ceremony of some kind, or it might even be your birth into a particular group – that leads to your starting a path or way. This is indicated by my wavy line. You have people to teach and guide you (indicated by the academic hats), and the path goes up and down according to your success in following the path. At death you then come to a final assessment, indicated by the scales of justice, where your life is scrutinised. Whether you are permitted to advance into a glorious world to come depends on your good deeds outweighing your bad ones.

'Since it is a merit-based system, no matter how good your teachers, advisers, gurus, imams, priests or rabbis are, they cannot guarantee you success at the final assessment. In other words, it is in a way very like a university course: you have to satisfy certain initial requirements, you follow the course and then sit the final examinations. However, no matter how good and kind your professors and teachers are, they cannot guarantee you a degree since that depends entirely on your merit at the final exams. Would it be fair to put it like that?'

The two men agreed that this was not only what they believed but that it was what *all* religious people believed. This was the essence of religion.

'Well then,' I said, 'that means that I am not a religious person.'

'But you said you were a Christian,' they replied.

'Yes, I am a Christian. What I now need to say is in direct answer to your original question: what is the difference between what I believe and what you believe?

'But let me say first that religions and philosophies have much moral teaching in common. Take, for example, what is often called the Golden Rule, one version of which says, "Treat others in the same way you would like them to treat you." You will find that in every religion and philosophy under the sun, including those religions and philosophies that do not believe in gods of any kind.

'The differences arise in what religions have to say not so much about morality but about how you relate to God or the gods. My illustration shows the common view that you share with many others. However, the Christian message is very different. It does *not* consist in a merit-based acceptance by God at the final judgement. Christianity teaches something utterly radical at this point. It tells us that we can be accepted at the beginning of the path. It teaches that the initial step is not a rite, ritual or ceremony performed on an infant or adult. Instead, it is a step of deliberate commitment to a person, Jesus Christ, that involves believing that he is God incarnate who came into the world to give his life as a ransom for our sins. He did so because our sins alienate us from God.'

At this point I drew a cross in the doorway at the beginning of my sketch in the dust. 'Now,' I remarked them, 'if you want my answer to your question, please listen and try to understand it before passing judgement on it.'

'Carry on,' they responded.

'Here is what Jesus said: "whoever hears my word and believes him who sent me has eternal life. He does not come into judgement, but has passed from death to life" (John 5:24). The context for these words is Jesus' astounding claim that he is going to be the final Judge of humankind.'

I turned to the judge in the window seat. 'Your Honour,' I asked. 'Suppose I presented my case to you, and you declared me to be free. Would I be right to believe you?'

He showed a burst of indignation. 'Of course,' he said. 'I am the judge, the final assessor. If I say you are free, then you are free.'

'Well, that is exactly it,' I replied. 'Jesus is the highest-level Judge in the universe. And he says that if we trust him personally, he will declare us to be right with God. This is on the grounds that he has himself paid, on the cross, the penalty of the guilty verdict that our sins merit. Moreover, we have evidence that this is true. As the early Christian apostle Paul stated to the philosophers at Athens, God has given assurance to all that this is so by raising Jesus from the dead (Acts 17:31).'

There was silence in the carriage for quite a while. Then the ambassador said to the judge, 'There is a great difference'. Turning to me he added, 'And it all depends on who Jesus Christ really is.'

'Exactly,' I replied.

They then told me their story. That weekend they had been attending a high-level conference in Vienna and found they had a day free. They asked for an embassy car to take them to Budapest. After spending most of the day there, they started on the return journey. Their car broke down just outside the train station. They had no option but to take the train.

'We don't travel by train,' they explained. 'We haven't been in one for years. Then we meet you on the train and have a conversation of a kind we have never experienced – not even in the leading universities in the world that we have attended. How do you account for that?'

'Very simply,' I responded. 'I think there is such a thing as divine guidance, and this is an example of it.'

I often wondered what happened to them but never found out. We witness. We sow the seed. In many cases that is all that we have the opportunity to do. We must then leave the rest to the Lord.

I relate this story to provide you with an illustration to share with your friends since a key aspect of our witness about the gospel is explaining the difference between conventional views of religion and Christianity. Perhaps you may feel intimidated by the idea of engaging in a similar conversation. However, God can and does use everyone as witnesses – not just professors or academics, nor only those trained as evangelists and apologists. Explaining how different Christianity is from other religions is something we can all do, in our own words and with our own methods, if we are willing to be bold.

This story also helps make another important point. God does not just 'exist' in an academic, philosophical way. He is alive and active in the world, working in our lives, reaching out to us, speaking to us through creation and ultimately through his Son, Jesus Christ. I have had far too many 'coincidences' in my life to put down to blind luck; this was just one of many. As you witness to your friends, you will find the same and it will bring you great joy.

7

EXPLAINING SALVATION

I have often used the picture that I drew on the floor of the train in order to explain what the term 'religion' means. I sometimes reinforce its message by amplifying it with another illustration. I hope that you will also find it as helpful as I have done, this time to make clear what salvation means.

Years ago I met a girl called Sally, fell in love with her and decided to propose to her. I approached her and gave her a gift-wrapped parcel. She asked what it was. I told her to open it and I would explain. She found in it a popular cookery book, expressed her appreciation and asked what it was for. I informed her that the book was full of rules and instructions on how to do excellent cooking. I then explained that I really loved her and would like her to be my wife on the following condition: if she kept its rules and instructions, cooking for me to a very high standard for, say, the next forty years! I continued that if she could do this, I would think about accepting her as my wife. If not, she could go home to her mother!

Of course, that is not how I proposed. It is an absurd scenario. Such a proposal would be insulting to her as a person in the extreme. It would suggest that I am going to wait for years to see how she performs in the kitchen before accepting her.

We would never dream of treating someone like that, would we? That is not how relationships are formed. Yet the remarkable thing is that this is precisely the attitude many people take towards God. They try to pile up their merit in the hope of one day gaining God's acceptance, as in my previous illustration of the wavy path. Anyone can see this method doesn't work with our fellow men and women. It won't work with God either, since God is the person in whose image we are made. However, often our pride hides this from us. It is remarkable how many people seem to be prepared to work for God to earn their salvation, yet are not prepared to trust him.

At the heart of salvation is the magnificent doctrine of the grace of God (Ephesians 2:4–5). It is worth stressing once more that when the Bible speaks of 'salvation', it means exactly that – a supremely loving action on the part of God to rescue those who could not help themselves. Without Jesus, we are 'dead' in our sins (Ephesians 2:1) and facing God's wrath (John 3:36). If we trust Jesus, we can be forgiven and find a new life and friendship with God – whoever we are and whatever we have done.

This brings us to another essential ingredient in the Christian message – and one which I mentioned in my illustration to the lawyers on the train: Jesus will be the final Judge. Christ himself claimed that role during his life on earth and said this about how the judgement would operate: 'For God did not send his Son into the world to condemn the world, but in order that the world might be saved through him. Whoever believes in him is not condemned, but whoever does not believe is condemned already, because he has not believed in the name of the only Son of God' (John 3:17–18).

People who think they can gain acceptance with God by their merit are clearly not aware of how they stand in view of God's judgement. All of us know that we fall short, sometimes very far short, of our own standards. God's standard is perfection. The more we take God's commands seriously, the more we see just how sinful we are. And yet many people hope that when it comes to God's final judgement, God will have a relaxed attitude and gloss over our misdeeds and accept us. They think God won't take his standards too seriously. This viewpoint fails to see that God's holiness cannot and will not be compromised. Since his standard is perfection, 'whoever keeps the whole law but fails in one point has become accountable for all of it' (James 2:10). If we then protest that this is not fair, it is like saying that it is not fair if, when only one link in the chain that connects a ship to its anchor, breaks, the whole ship goes adrift and is lost. It is in the nature of the relationship that this is so.

The only way to avoid judgement, as Christ in his love tells us, is to cease trying to gain acceptance by merit and instead trust Jesus for salvation. Acceptance with God does not depend on attainment of a standard of perfection. In any case, that is humanly impossible to attain. The good news is that the salvation by which God is prepared to accept us, as the New Testament repeatedly says, is given by God's grace as a gift: 'For by grace you have been saved through faith. And this is not your own doing; it is the gift of God, not a result of works, so that no one may boast' (Ephesians 2:8–9).

However, like all gifts, salvation has to be received. It is not automatically credited to us. Rather, it involves our repentance. It also requires us, as a deliberate act of our will, to put our trust in God for our salvation. The logic of this is important. The original human rebellion against God (Genesis 3) involved Adam's and Eve's lack of trust and grasping at independence. Therefore the way back for all humans to have a relationship with God inevitably involves repenting of that same attitude, and instead trusting God and learning to depend on him.

We therefore need to tell our friends that salvation depends on the following:

1. REPENTANCE

We must have a change of heart and mind. We need to face the fact that we are sinners who have offended God by rebelling against him and his rules. We have to agree with God's guilty verdict on the sin in our lives. Then we have to turn away from our sinful lifestyle.

2. FAITH

We have to believe that Jesus lovingly took upon himself the judgement we deserve for our sins. We must receive from him and trust in that gift of salvation, knowing that we could not earn or provide it for ourselves. That is a deliberate commitment. Some react to this by arguing that it cannot be true, for if salvation does not depend on our merit, we can carry on merrily living as we like and God will still accept us. This is not so. The person who takes that attitude shows that he or she has not begun to understand what repentance means. There is no salvation for anyone who intends to keep on sinning.

We said above that in marriage acceptance occurs at the beginning of the relationship. It is the same with Christ. We are accepted the moment we repent and trust him. From then on, we wish to live to please the Lord, not in order to gain his acceptance but because we already have been given it. To do otherwise shows that we have never grasped or treasured what salvation really means.

Many people, when they are ready to take this step, appreciate being led in a prayer of commitment. If that is the case, you may like to use the following:

Lord Jesus Christ, I present myself to you now.

I know I have sinned in my thoughts, words and actions. I am very conscious of my sin, my need for your forgiveness. I am truly sorry.

I know that I cannot obtain your acceptance by anything that I can do. But I thank you that you came from heaven to save me – by giving your life upon the cross for me and by rising again.

As best as I understand, and gratefully, I give my life back to you, asking for your forgiveness and your acceptance. Please come fully into my life as I trust you alone for my salvation.

Come in as my Saviour to cleanse me.

Come in as my Lord to control me.

Come in as my Friend to be with me.

Please send the Holy Spirit to live inside me and make me a child in your family.

I am stepping out in faith and in total trust of Christ.

Amen.

It is also helpful for us to point out that this commitment may not necessarily be accompanied by any special feelings. Since Christianity is true and Jesus is the Son of God, we can rely on his Word that if we trust him, we receive eternal life. That is a matter of fact, not feeling. Therefore, although some may at once feel joy, for others the joy comes later. Once a person commits themselves in marriage, they are married whether they always feel like it or not!

WHAT IF I FEEL 'TOO BUSY' TO WITNESS TO OTHERS?

We live in a very highly pressurised society, particularly during our working lives. Many of us are so busy with work that we come home with scarcely enough energy to help at home, let alone to get involved in reaching out to our neighbours. What makes these competing pressures worse sometimes is when we are challenged to witness by means of the kind of stories we have seen in this book. We simply don't have the time to share *The Word: One to One* with seven people each week, and we don't tend to meet people that are easy to talk to.

That scenario may well be true for you, and I do not wish to deny its difficulties. However, there is a world of difference between doing nothing and doing something. How can we overcome a 'natural' lethargy and get involved in evangelism? Well, I am assuming that the person reading this book is a Christian believer. So perhaps the first question we need to ask ourselves is: how did I become a believer? For most people the answer is well-known – through the witness of friends. In other words, someone had bothered. They took time to share the gospel message with you and the result was you received new spiritual life. Not only that, but that person told you that Jesus the Lord had bothered. He had bothered to come to earth in human form and, above all, had bothered to die on the cross for your sins, because he loved you. So you are eternally indebted to people that bothered.

Given this, it would now sound rather strange for you to turn round and say, 'I can't really be bothered to witness about Jesus.' In fact, to be blunt, it raises a very serious question: what do you really think being a Christian is? It means being a follower of Jesus as Lord, and that means being prepared to do as he says. One of those things is to go into all the world to share the message that has been shared with you.

The vital thing is to get involved. Start small and watch how the Lord begins to enrich your life. Then, instead of feeling like not bothering about evangelism, you will look out for every opportunity to see Jesus work in your life.

ENCOURAGING SOMEONE TO GROW AS A CHRISTIAN

To those who have trusted Christ through our witness, we can rejoice with them that they have received eternal life (John 3:16). They have been born into God's family (John 1:12–13). Like all newborn babies, though, they need to feed in order to grow.

That means that they need to start (if they have not already done so) reading the Bible for themselves as a daily priority. Since you have been witnessing to them, it is highly appropriate – and you will find it very rewarding – to make time to meet with them and read the Bible together. This will give you the opportunity to introduce them to many of the good Bible reading aids that are available.

It is important, however, since they are now part of God's family, that they should meet with other Christians to encourage one another (Hebrews 10:24–25). Therefore help them find a welcoming church that is committed to the teaching of Scripture. It is also helpful to encourage them to become involved in a Bible study group. Here they will find a smaller network of caring friends with whom it is easier to relate to, discuss the Bible and pray with. It might be that they are married to a fellow believer. If so, it is important that their faith becomes central to their marriage, including by reading the Bible and praying with their spouses. Many couples – including those who are busy – have found *Our Daily Bread* notes, published by Our Daily Bread Ministries and now available online, helpful in doing this in a relaxed way.

It is important to prepare new Christians for the fact that, despite their commitment to pleasing God, they will inevitably sin. No one of us is perfect this side of heaven. We are a work in progress. Facing that ongoing process of transformation can be uncomfortable at times. Assure them that once we have received eternal life, we will never come into penal judgement (John 5:24). When we subsequently sin, it does not mean that we may lose our salvation and be cast out of God's family. God's promise is that we will be forgiven because of what Christ has already done for us (1 John 1:5–10). However, we need to be honest before God, confessing our sin to him (1 John 1:9). Scripture gives many examples of this. See, for instance, Psalm 51, which is one of King David's prayers of confession.

Another important aspect to highlight for new believers is that they will need to develop their Christian character. God supplies his children with all the resources needed to do that but it will not happen automatically without our co-operation (2 Peter 1:3–15). Furthermore, if we do not co-operate with the Lord in this process, precisely because he loves us, he will discipline us for the sake of our character development (Hebrews 12:6–11).

We need also to encourage people who have just become Christians to begin to explore the potential of the life they have received as a gift from God and to set themselves to work for him. This is not to gain acceptance with him but because God has accepted them and has 'created' them 'for good works' (Ephesians 2:10). All sorts of new possibilities open up – learning to be stewards of their time, their money and their varied gifts. By being involved in a church, this will allow others to help them discover what opportunities they have in now working for Christ's kingdom.

There is nothing more fulfilling than seeing God working in the lives of those people to whom we are witnessing. Seeing them cross the line from darkness into light, from death to life, and subsequently demonstrating the reality of their conversion in their lives, is one of life's richest experiences for a Christian. My prayer, as I come to the end of this little book, is that it may be your experience too.

NOTES

1. Lennox, J.C., *Can Science Explain Everything?* (Good Book Company, 2019).

2. These podcasts can be found at Premier Christian Radio website: http://bit.ly/2xHZgXX

3. *The Word: One to One* is available in four volumes (10Publishing, 2014).

4. Rico Tice's introduction to *The Word: One to One* can be found at: http://bit.ly/word121

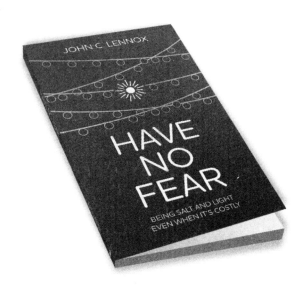

a division of 10 of those.com

10Publishing is the publishing house of **10ofThose**. It is committed to producing quality Christian resources that are biblical and accessible.

www.10ofthose.com is our online retail arm selling thousands of quality books at discounted prices.

For information contact: **info@10ofthose.com** or check out our website: **www.10ofthose.com**